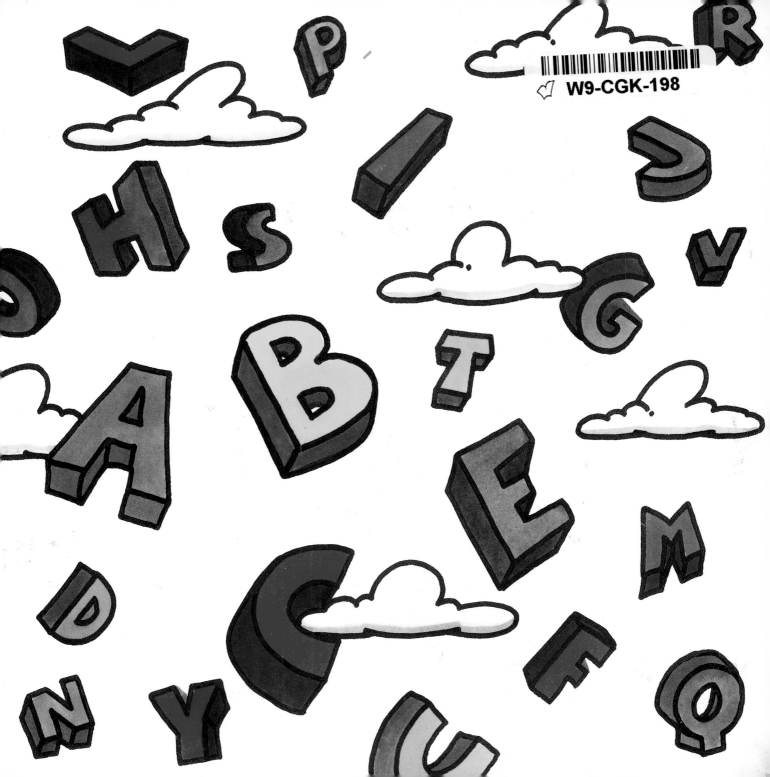

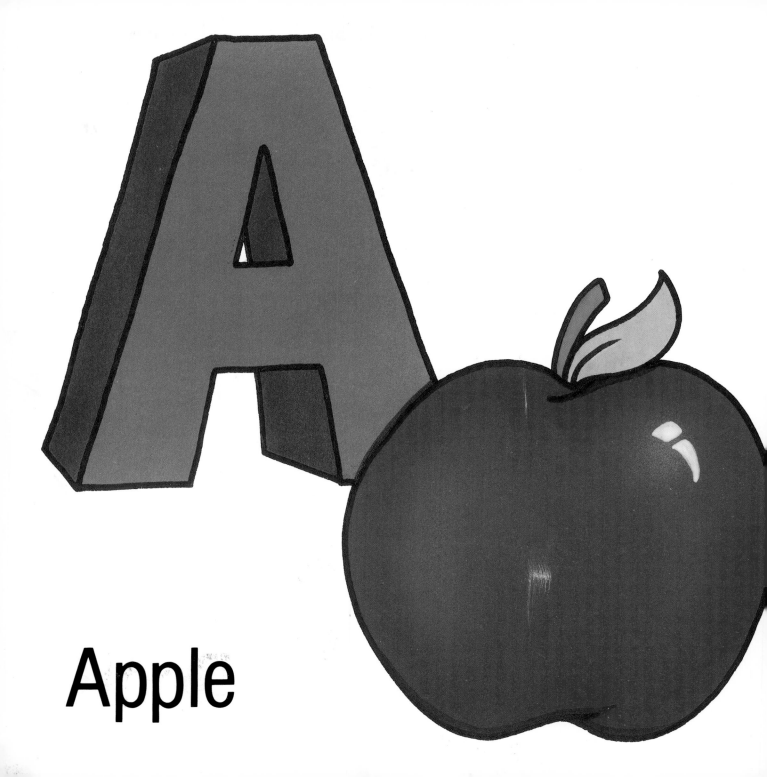

Apple

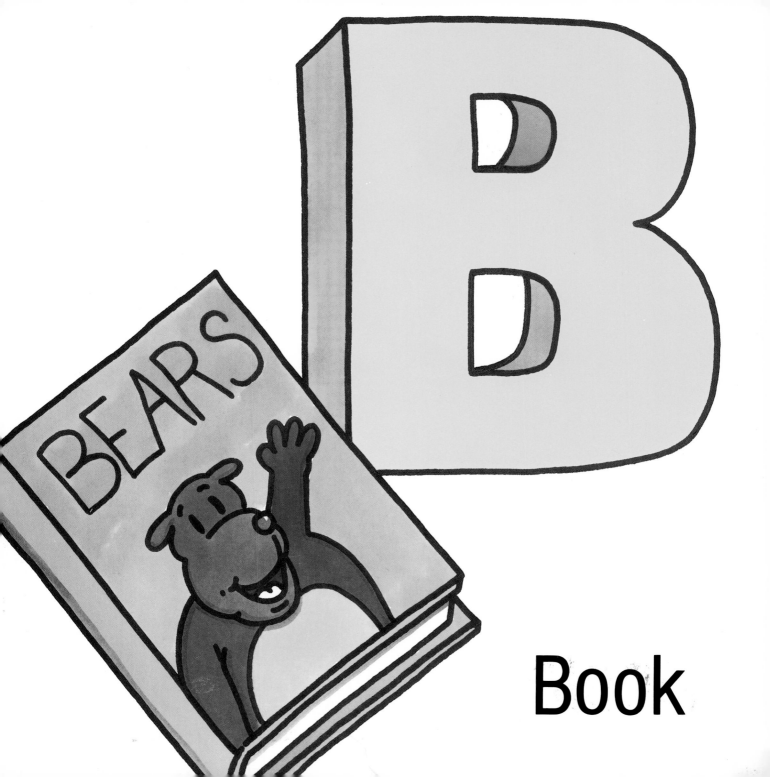

Book

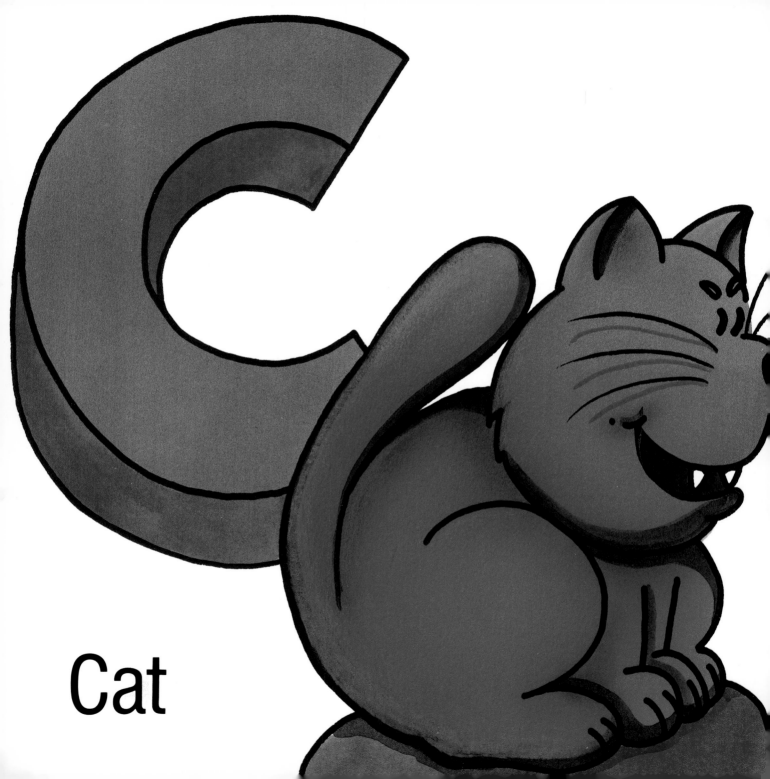

Cat

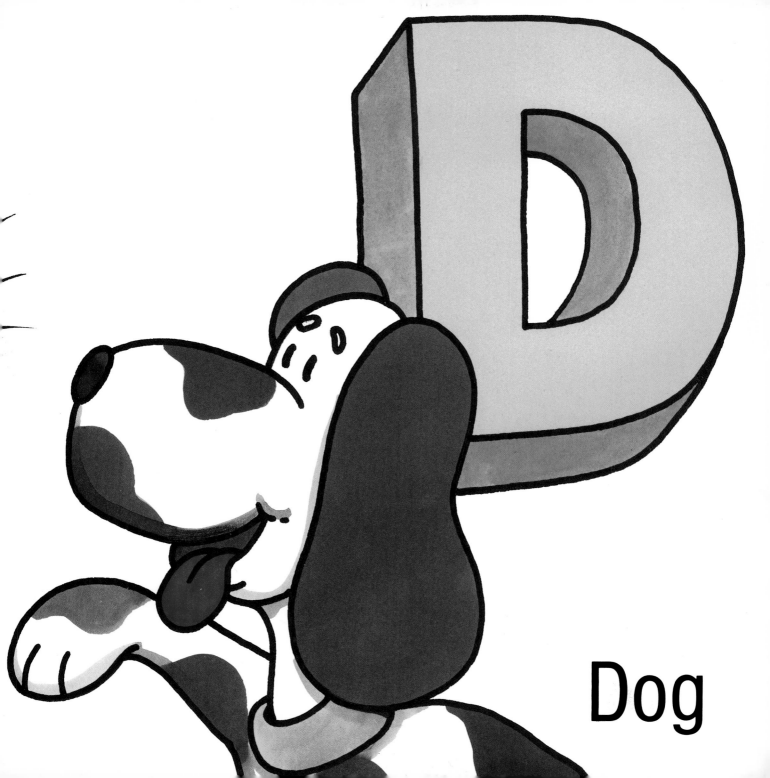

Dog

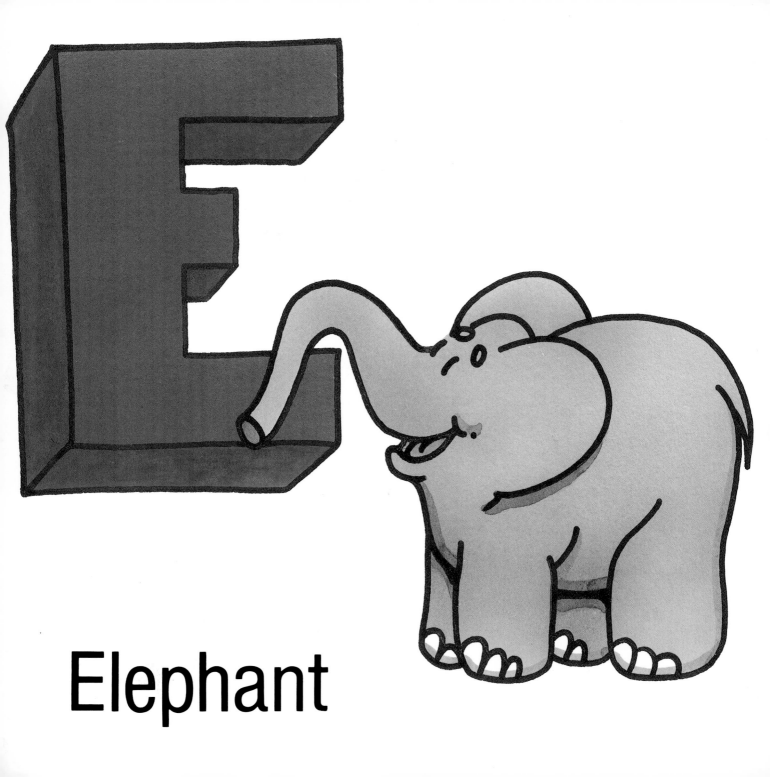

Elephant

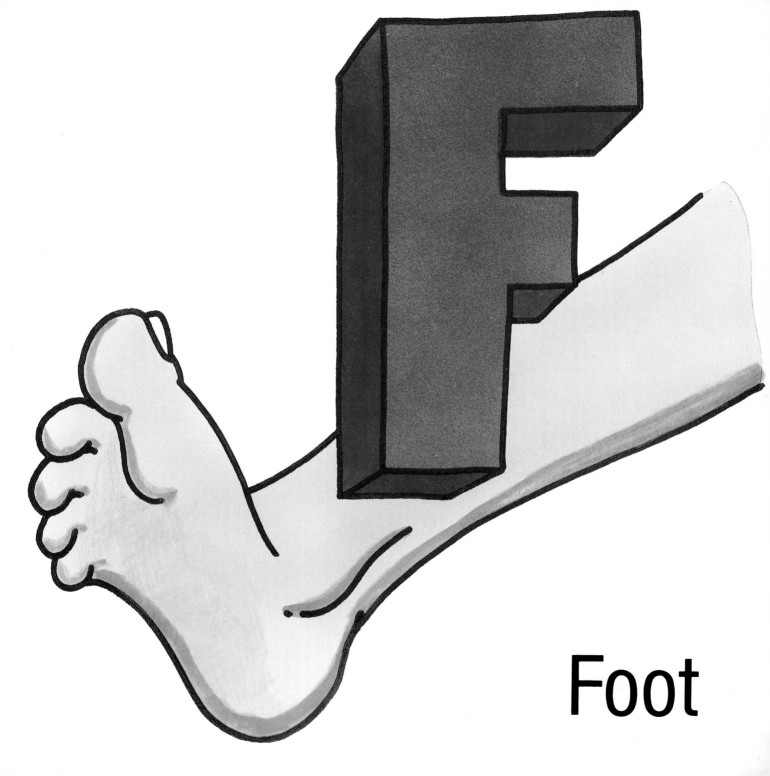

Foot

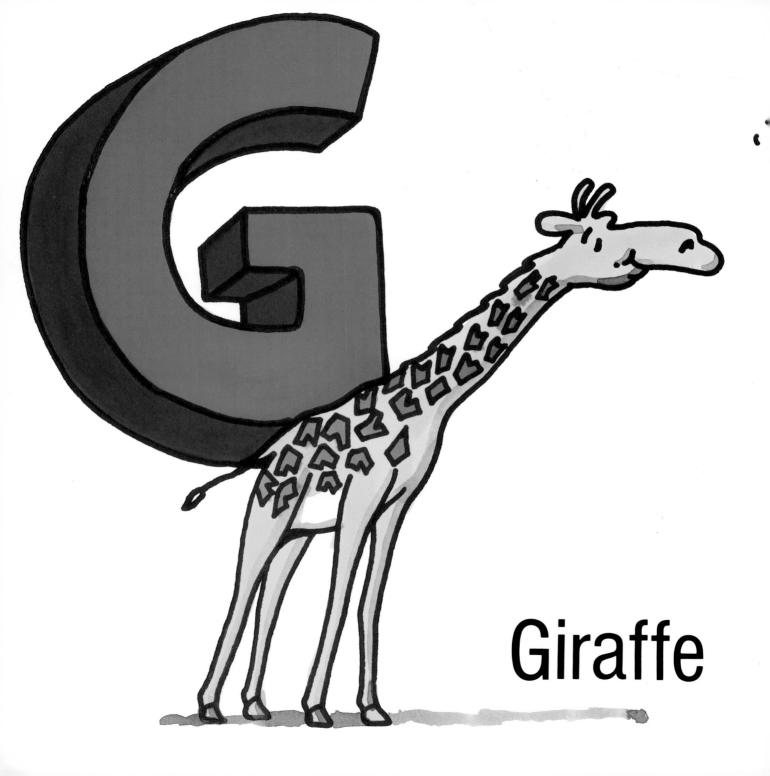

Giraffe

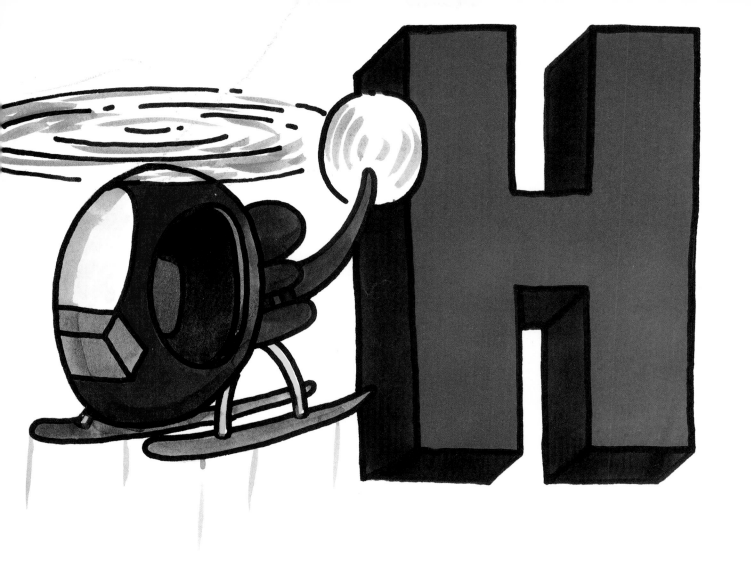

Helicopter

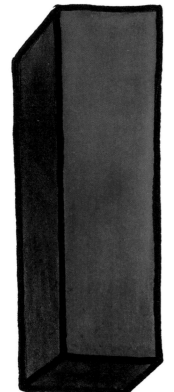

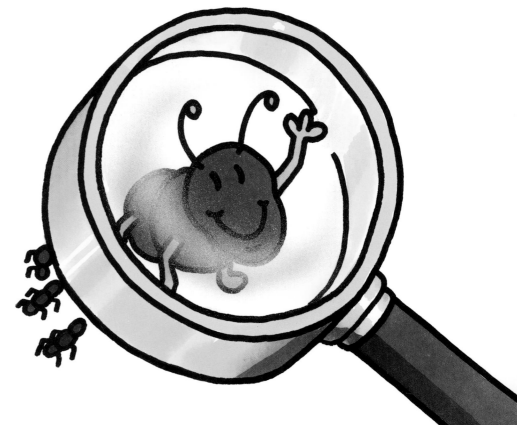

Insect

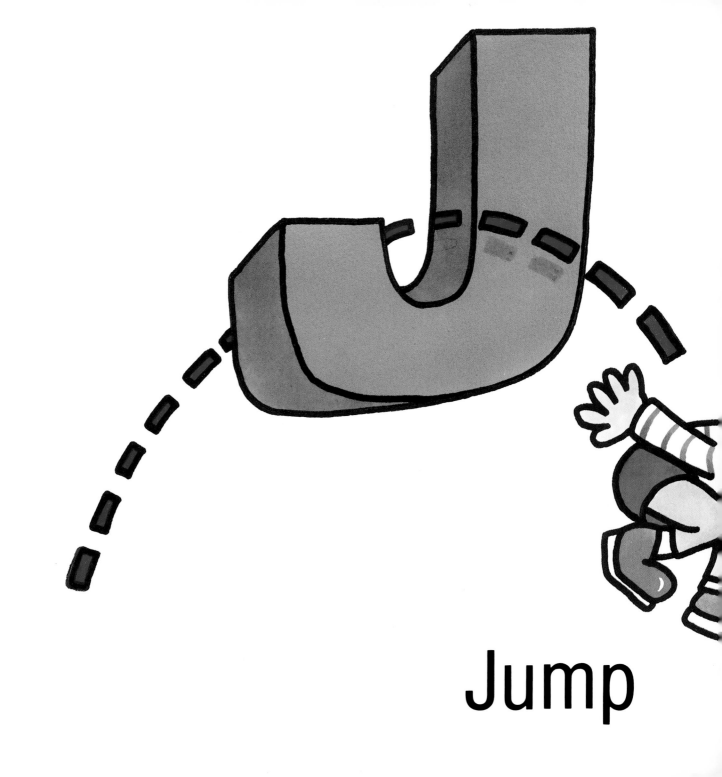

Jump

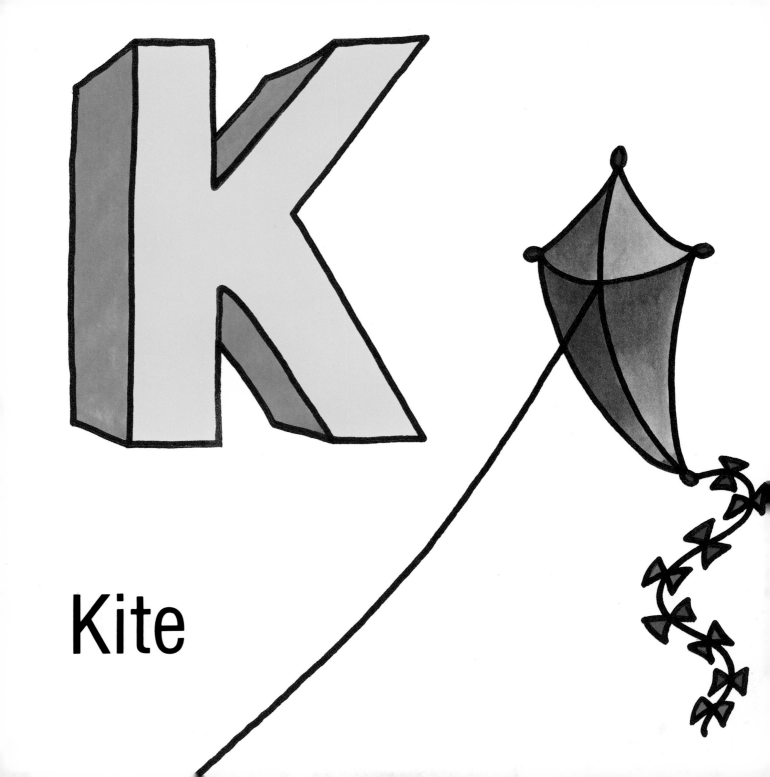

Kite

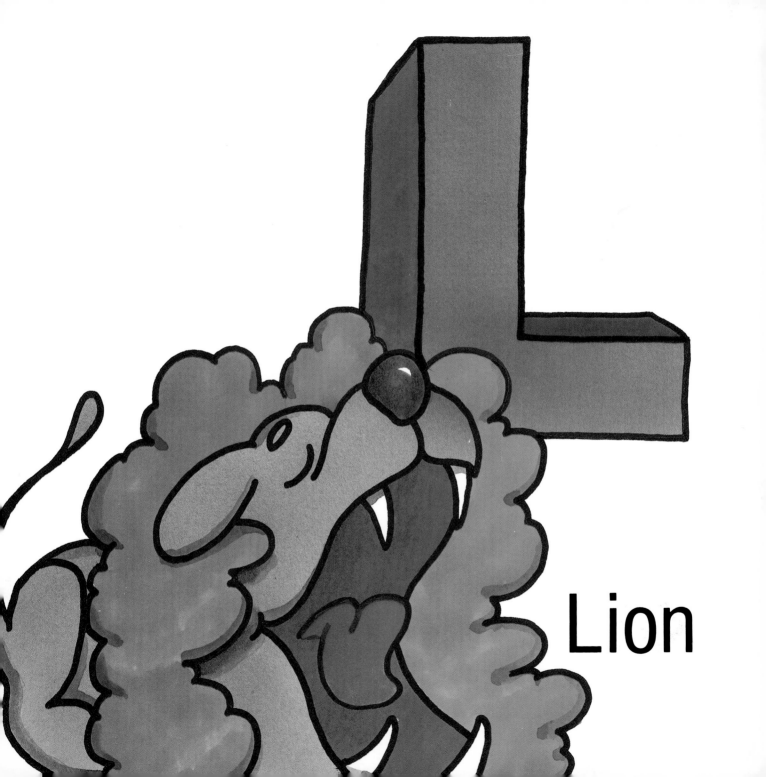

Lion

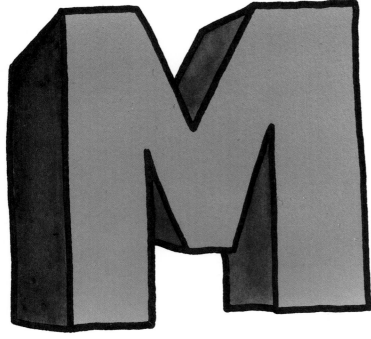

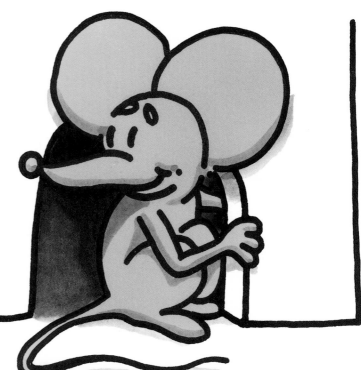

Mouse

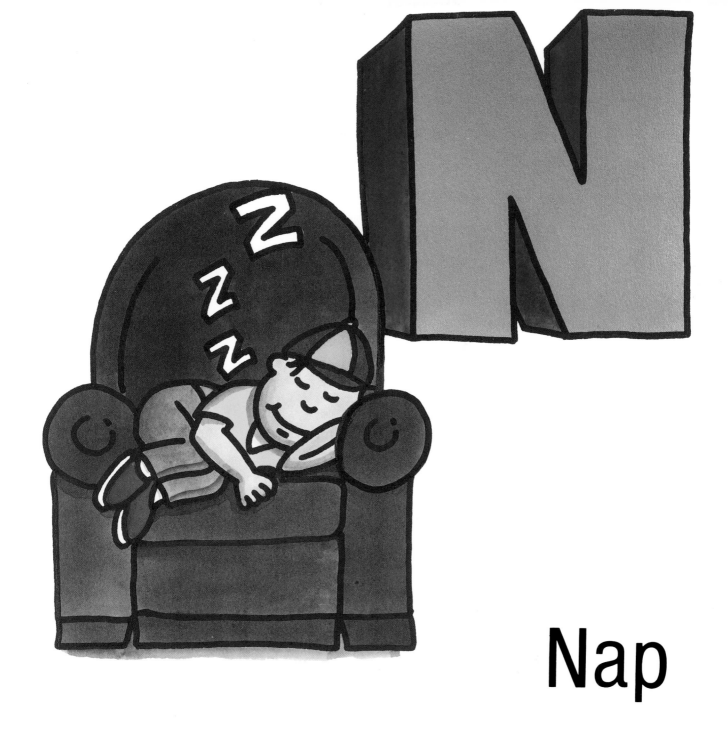

Nap

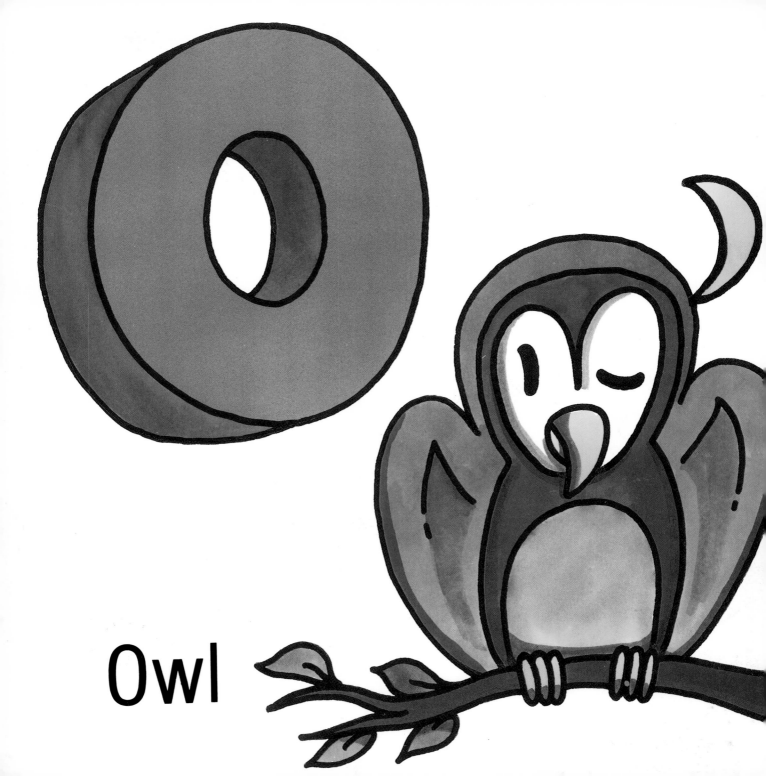

Owl

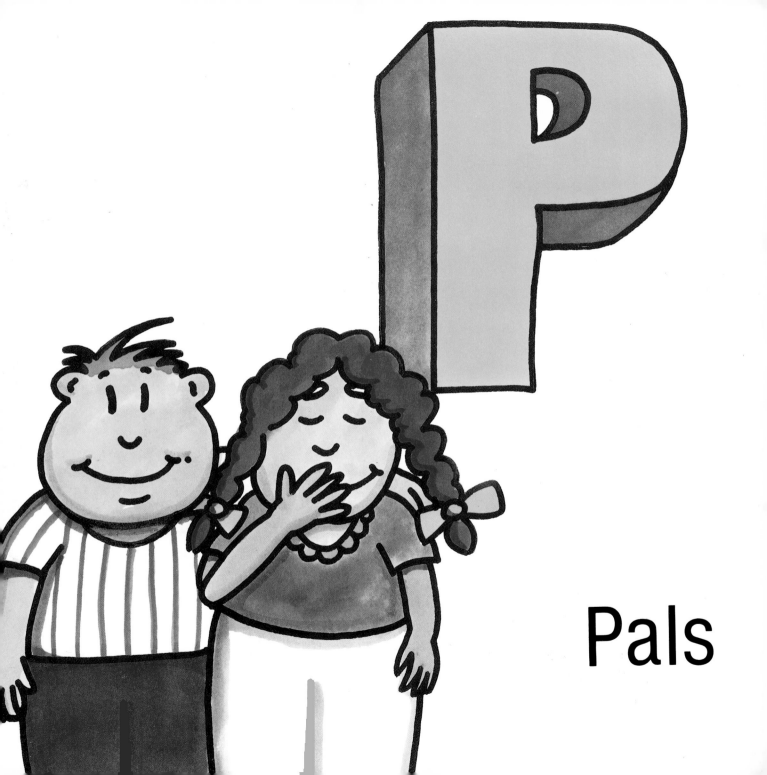

Pals

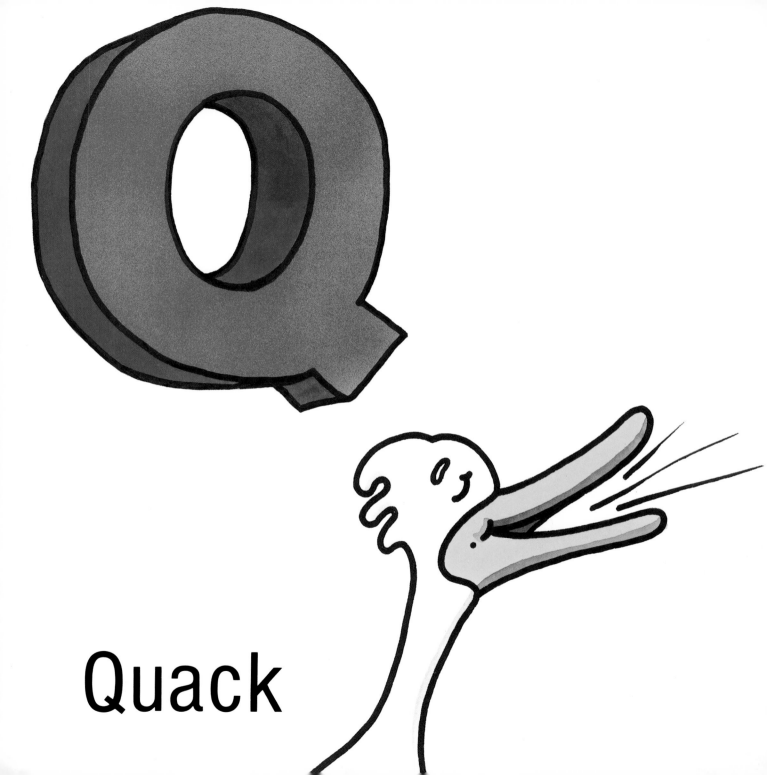

Quack

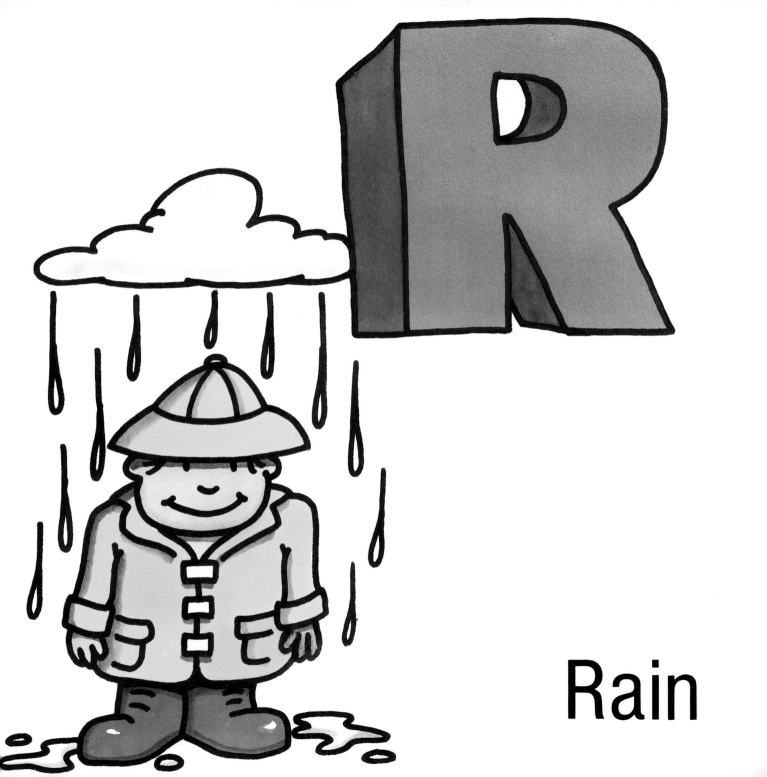

Rain

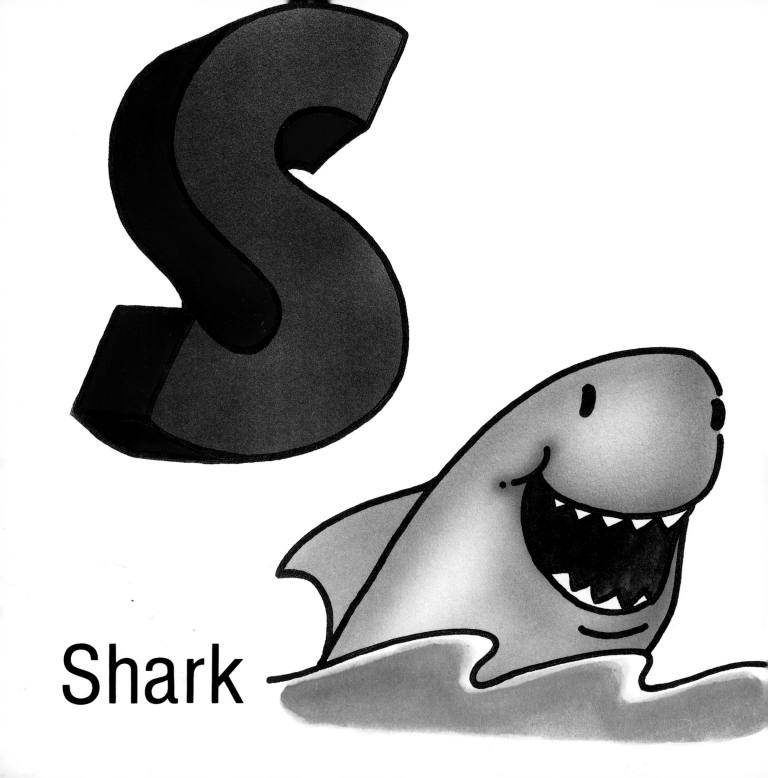

Shark

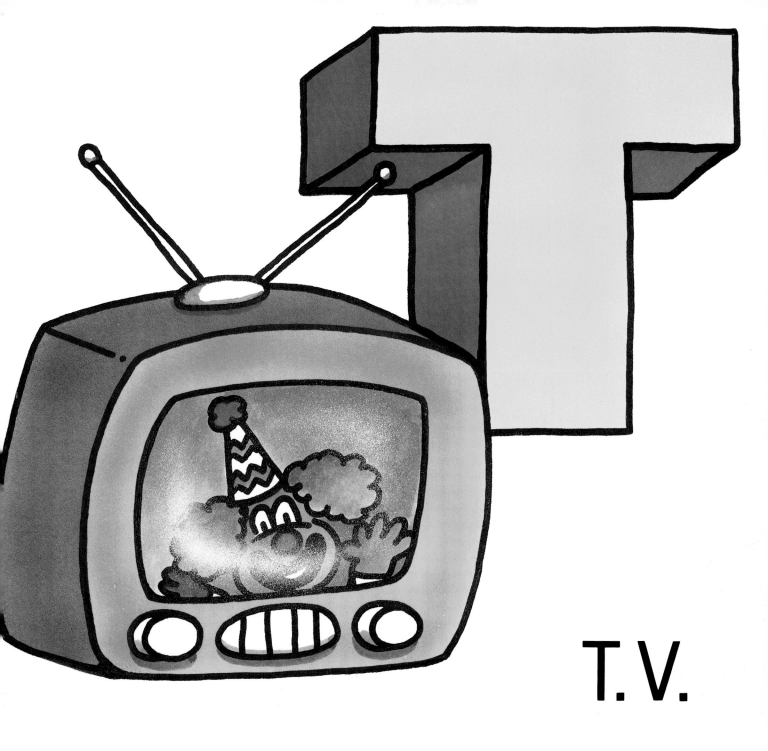

T.V.

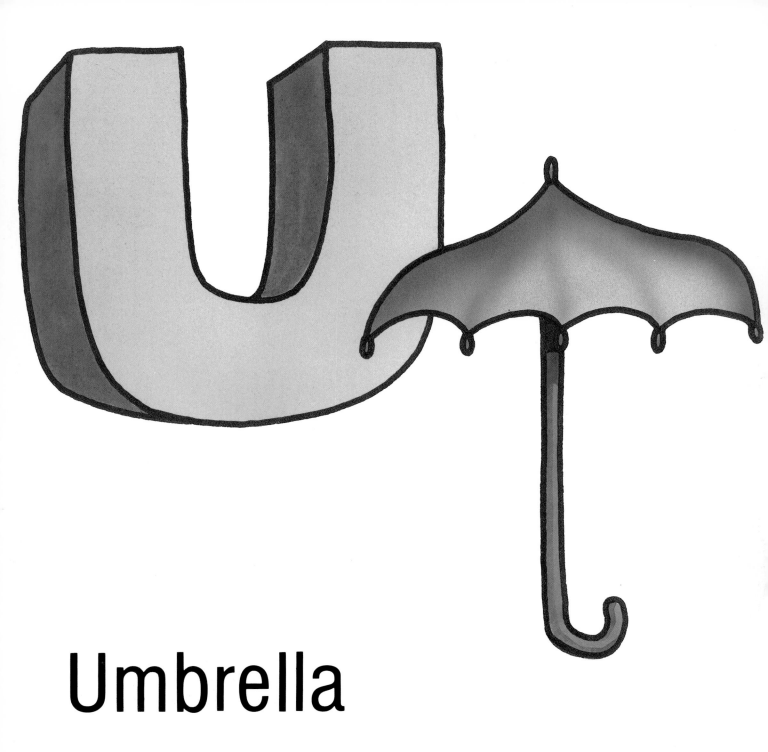

Umbrella

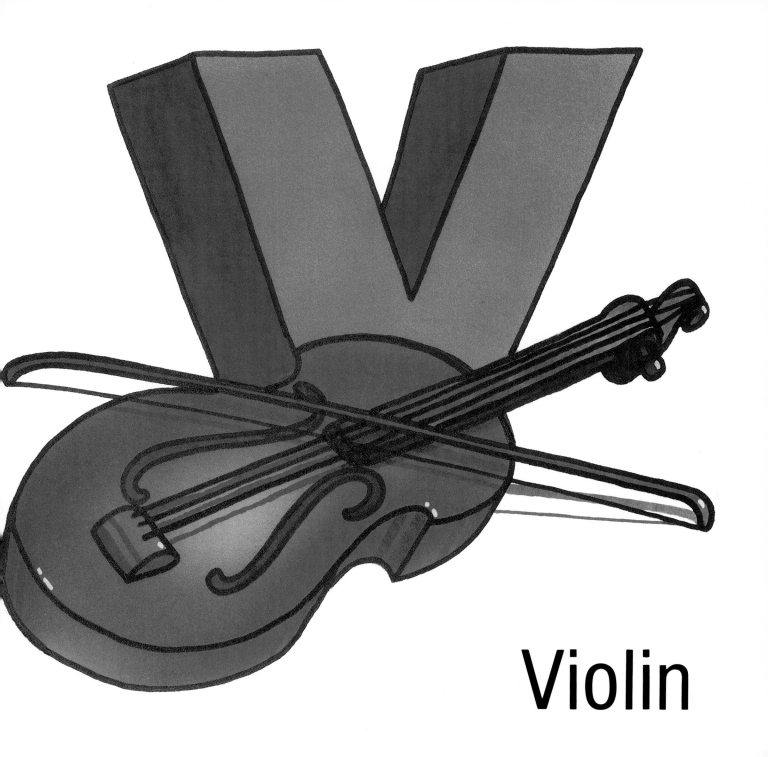

Violin

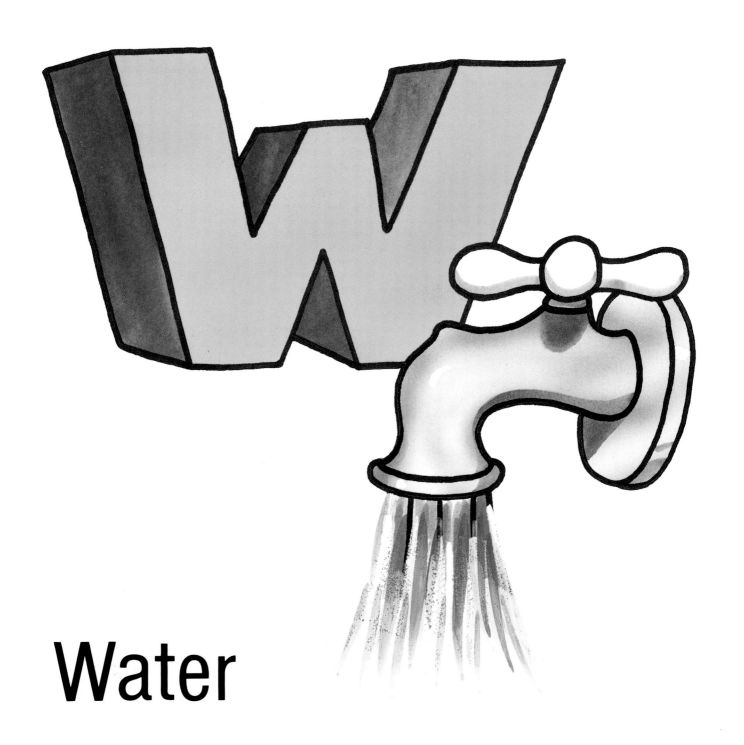

Water

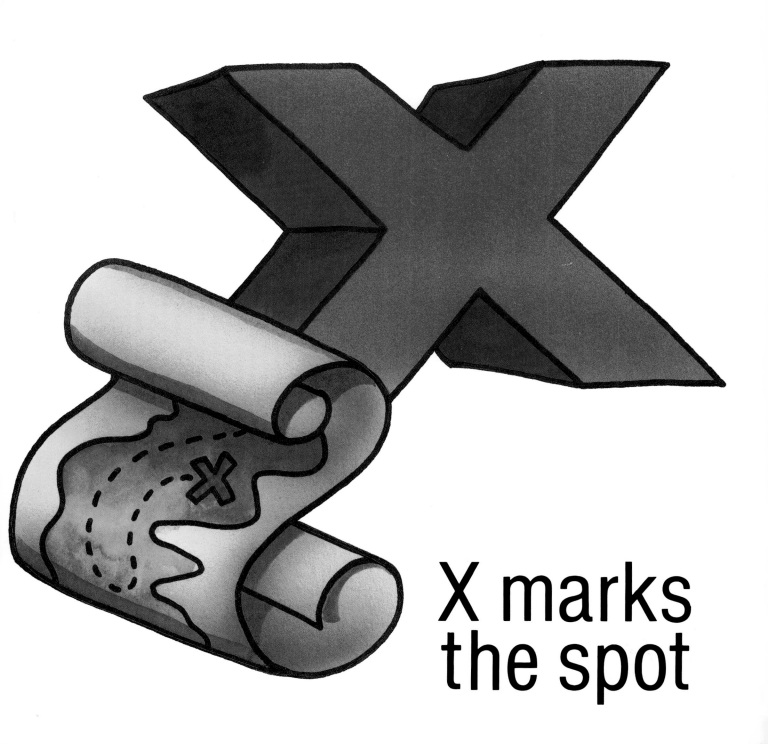

X marks
the spot

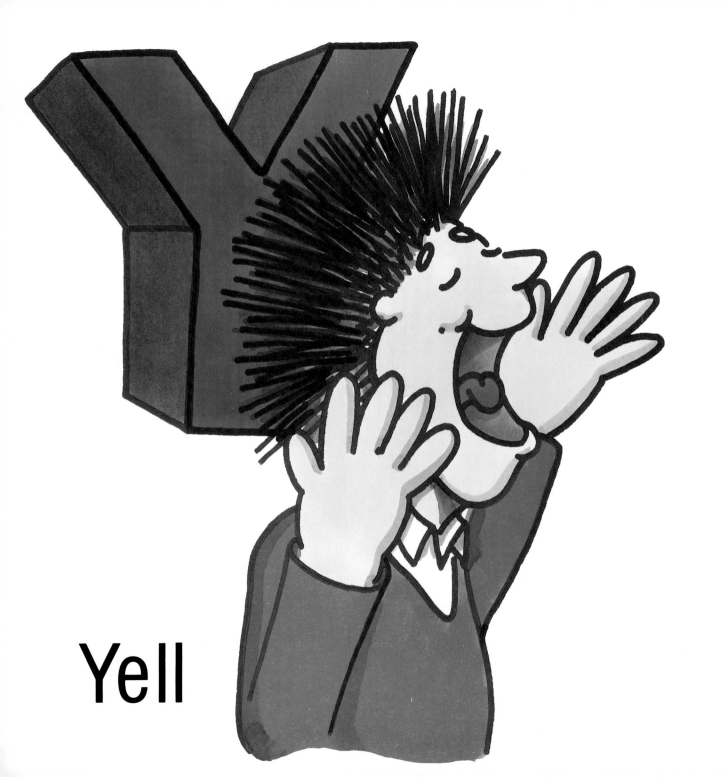

Yell

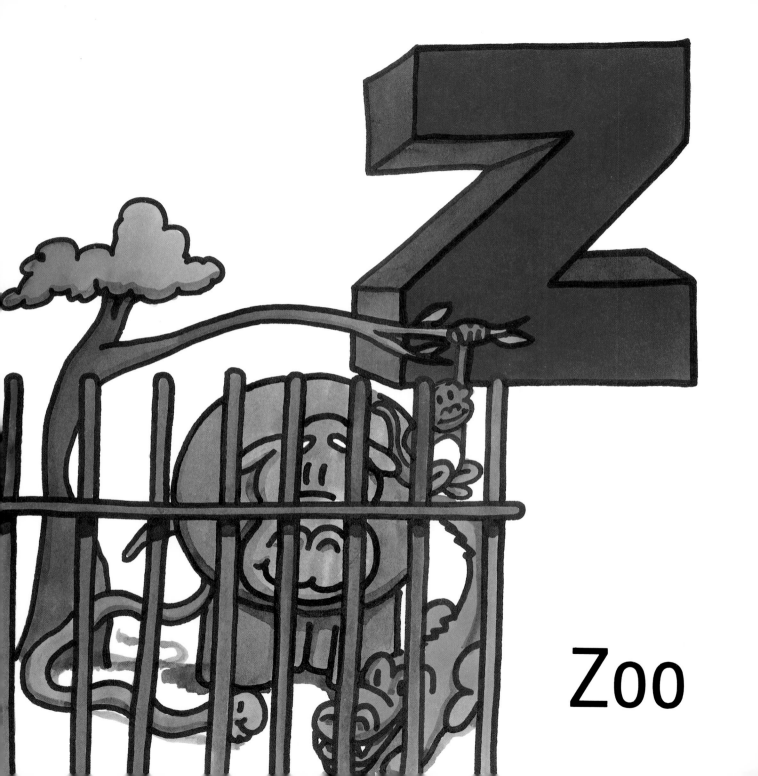

Zoo

ABCD

JKLM

STUV